Distinguished Wisdom Presents . . .
"GAIN 20/20 VISION FOR THE NEW DECADE"
2025 – 365 DAY JOURNAL

Document Your Journey!

Pastor Terrance Levise Turner, MBA

Well Spoken Inc. | *Nashville, TN.*

© 2025 Terrance Levise Turner
All rights reserved. No part of this publication may be reproduced, scanned, transmitted or distributed in any printed or electronic or mechanical forms or methods, including photocopying, recording, or other without prior written permission of the publisher, except in the case of brief select quotations embodied in critical reviews and certain other noncommercial uses permitted by copyright law. For permission requests, write to the publisher, addressed below.

Unless otherwise indicated, all Scripture quotations are taken from the King James Version of the Bible.

Well Spoken Inc.
P.O. Box 291806 Nashville, TN. 37229
WellSpokenInc@bellsouth.net
www.TerranceTurnerLivingProverbs.com

Ordering Information
Quantity sales. Special discounts are available on quantity purchases by corporations, associations, and others. For details, contact the "Special Sales Department" at the address above.

Cover design by Susan of LSDdesign/99Designs.com
Book design by Terrance Levise Turner
Printed in the United States of America
ISBN 9781734482089 Paperback

Introduction

The Benefits of Journaling

Journaling has so many benefits for you, such as reducing anxiety in today's circumstances and uncertainty in society. God can give you answers as you take time to meditate upon His Word and let Him bring clarity to your mind. This journal gives you the opportunity to capture your thoughts and ideas as you pursue your goals. Journaling gives you hope for the future as you consider the good things that God does for you everyday. Journaling allows you to develop a "thankfulness record." You can keep track of the various blessings and goodness that God shows you, big and small. This will bring more joy in your life and help you to have a grateful and more peaceful perspective. Journaling also allows you to discover a brighter perspective regarding areas of your life that you may not have thought of before. As you read the book **Gain 20/20 Vision For The New Decade! A Step By Step Path To A More Successful Future!** you will discover principles you will want to take notes on how to apply. You will also want to reflect further on your goals that you write down in the **Gain 20/20 Vision For The New Decade! 10-Year Calendar 2020-2030: A Decade of Achievement!** You will want to further document your discoveries over the next decade on how planning and goal-setting changes your life. Please enjoy writing in this journal for the entire year. You will create a valuable record of your treasured thoughts. You will be so glad that you decided to "Document Your Journey!"

Gain 20/20 Vision For The New Decade!
2025 – 365 Day Journal
Document Your Journey!

Living Proverb #2: "Don't fight change. A changing life is a living life. The only people who don't change are the dead."

Gain 20/20 Vision For The New Decade!
2025 – 365 Day Journal
Document Your Journey!

Living Proverb #5: "Hurry, worry, and anxiety are clear indicators that your life's priorities are out of alignment."

Gain 20/20 Vision For The New Decade!
2025 – 365 Day Journal
Document Your Journey!

Living Proverb #8: "Don't be so anxious to run out on the field of life each day without reading the playbook-the Bible."

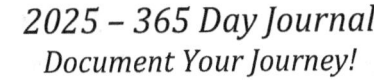

Gain 20/20 Vision For The New Decade!
2025 – 365 Day Journal
Document Your Journey!

Living Proverb #9: "A wise old owl sat on an oak. The more he saw, the less he spoke. The less he spoke, the more he heard. Why can't we be like that wise old bird."

Gain 20/20 Vision For The New Decade!
2025 – 365 Day Journal
Document Your Journey!

Living Proverb #15: "We must often take the time to seek the Lord until we get down to the ground floor of our lives in order to truly see where we stand."

Gain 20/20 Vision For The New Decade!
2025 – 365 Day Journal
Document Your Journey!

Living Proverb #16: "Prayer is the highlight of the day!"

Gain 20/20 Vision For The New Decade!
2025 – 365 Day Journal
Document Your Journey!

Living Proverb #17: "Don't make the rational or expedient decision. Make the effective, immediate decision that the prevailing condition requires."

Gain 20/20 Vision For The New Decade!
2025 – 365 Day Journal
Document Your Journey!

Living Proverb #18: "There are two rules for helping people: Help them with a hand up. Help them with a ladder. A hand up provides support, and a ladder provides tools for change and steps to get there."

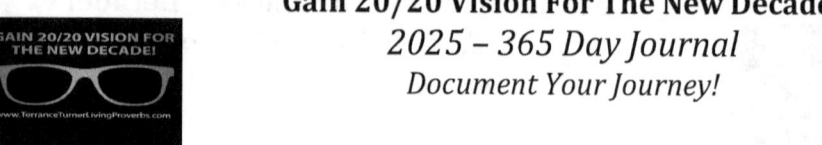

Gain 20/20 Vision For The New Decade!
2025 – 365 Day Journal
Document Your Journey!

Living Proverb #20: "Sufficient unto the day are the requirements thereof, and God's grace is sufficient for you for those requirements."

Gain 20/20 Vision For The New Decade!
2025 – 365 Day Journal
Document Your Journey!

Living Proverb #21: "The key to mastery is alone time, to grapple with the complexities of any art, science, skill, or knowledge base, whether it be the mastery of the violin or piano, understanding the complexities of stock trading, or the research and discovery of a cure or invention."

Gain 20/20 Vision For The New Decade!
2025 – 365 Day Journal
Document Your Journey!

Living Proverb #22: "Only you can decide to dedicate to the discipline of increasing in knowledge, wisdom, and skill. No one else can determine your habits. And no one else can determine your rewards."

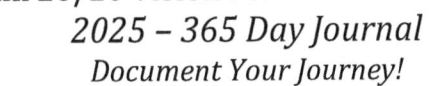

Gain 20/20 Vision For The New Decade!
2025 – 365 Day Journal
Document Your Journey!

Living Proverb #24: "If you stay where life is moving, you will move with life."

Gain 20/20 Vision For The New Decade!
2025 – 365 Day Journal
Document Your Journey!

Living Proverb #25: "If God is working in any area of your life, God is working in every area of your life. When your life is in God's hands, He leaves no area untouched."

Gain 20/20 Vision For The New Decade!
2025 – 365 Day Journal
Document Your Journey!

Living Proverb #28: "As the refining of silver and gold increases its beauty, value, attractiveness, and worth through the application of heat, so is a man or woman increased in value, beauty, profitability, potential, and worth through reading, study, practice, and discipline."

Gain 20/20 Vision For The New Decade!
2025 – 365 Day Journal
Document Your Journey!

Living Proverb #29: "Do not initiate behavior that is not sustainable or that promises no enduring reward."

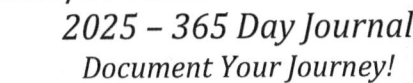

Gain 20/20 Vision For The New Decade!
2025 – 365 Day Journal
Document Your Journey!

Living Proverb #35: "If you want tomorrow, you must fight for it today!"

Gain 20/20 Vision For The New Decade!
2025 – 365 Day Journal
Document Your Journey!

Living Proverb #36: "God can trust you to organize your own time and seek your own provision. You don't need a boss, supervisor, or alarm clock to make you get up and be productive because you know winter is coming, and you've got to eat!"

Gain 20/20 Vision For The New Decade!
2025 – 365 Day Journal
Document Your Journey!

Living Proverb #38: "I declare God's notable favor upon you and yours. In Jesus Name, amen."

Gain 20/20 Vision For The New Decade!
2025 – 365 Day Journal
Document Your Journey!

Living Proverb #39: "Plan for tomorrow, but master today. Today's journey is your chief responsibility. Today's success creates the path for tomorrow's success and fulfillment."

Gain 20/20 Vision For The New Decade!
2025 – 365 Day Journal
Document Your Journey!

___

Living Proverb #40: "The degree of information that you gather on any subject of study will determine the eventual degree of formation that subject takes in your mind. You will then eventually see the big picture."

Gain 20/20 Vision For The New Decade!
2025 – 365 Day Journal
Document Your Journey!

Living Proverb #42: "Surround yourself with people who believe!"

Gain 20/20 Vision For The New Decade!
2025 – 365 Day Journal
Document Your Journey!

Living Proverb #40: "The degree of information that you gather on any subject of study will determine the eventual degree of formation that subject takes in your mind. You will then eventually see the big picture."

Gain 20/20 Vision For The New Decade!
2025 – 365 Day Journal
Document Your Journey!

Living Proverb #1068: "Every victory is a victory toward a greater victory. The best is ahead and is guaranteed!"

Gain 20/20 Vision For The New Decade!
2025 – 365 Day Journal
Document Your Journey!

Living Proverb #1072: "In order to live a full, rich, and abundant life, you must live your life like a *stingy accountant*! Account for every penny spent. Account for every moment spent."

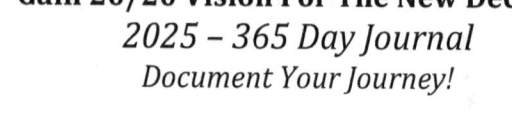

Gain 20/20 Vision For The New Decade!
2025 – 365 Day Journal
Document Your Journey!

Living Proverb #1073: "The key to unbroken success is unbroken focus."

Gain 20/20 Vision For The New Decade!
2025 – 365 Day Journal
Document Your Journey!

Living Proverb #1075: "If you keep on progressing, and keep on confessing, and keep on pressing, you will soon be possessing! Don't give up!"

Gain 20/20 Vision For The New Decade!
2025 – 365 Day Journal
Document Your Journey!

Living Proverb #1076: "Do not fear when faced with life's uncertainties. Remain in faith, and do the practical. The power of your faith is greater than your circumstances. Circumstances are subject to change. Faith is the power to change it."

Gain 20/20 Vision For The New Decade!
2025 – 365 Day Journal
Document Your Journey!

Living Proverb #1077: "The seed for your future is inside of you. God created you self-contained with everything you need. As you plant your potential to produce results, through your words, actions, and efforts, you will produce the future you were destined for from the beginning."

Gain 20/20 Vision For The New Decade!
2025 – 365 Day Journal
Document Your Journey!

Living Proverb #1078: "Sometimes stepping out in faith is to take the time necessary to get the knowledge needed to make a solid, informed move."

Gain 20/20 Vision For The New Decade!
2025 – 365 Day Journal
Document Your Journey!

Living Proverb #1079: "The Word works every time, if we will work every time."

Gain 20/20 Vision For The New Decade!
2025 – 365 Day Journal
Document Your Journey!

Living Proverb #1081: "The diamonds are in the details!"

Gain 20/20 Vision For The New Decade!
2025 – 365 Day Journal
Document Your Journey!

Living Proverb #1082: "Forget your troubles, and just enjoy the day!"

Gain 20/20 Vision For The New Decade!
2025 – 365 Day Journal
Document Your Journey!

Living Proverb #1086: "Every reality started as a dream."

Gain 20/20 Vision For The New Decade!
2025 – 365 Day Journal
Document Your Journey!

Living Proverb #1088: "Be sure to frame your day around spending time with God through reading the Bible and prayer. Do not limit the Lord to only a small piece, or escape hatch in your life. Rather, make Him the entire frame, foundation, and structure of your life."

Gain 20/20 Vision For The New Decade!
2025 – 365 Day Journal
Document Your Journey!

Living Proverb #1089: "As you start the day today, know that your Heavenly Father is good. His mercy endures forever, and He loves you! Have a great day!"

Gain 20/20 Vision For The New Decade!
2025 – 365 Day Journal
Document Your Journey!

Living Proverb #1090: "The bigger person gives grace. The bigger person gives forgiveness. The bigger person gives patience. The bigger person is more like God. Be the bigger person. Be like God."

Gain 20/20 Vision For The New Decade!
2025 – 365 Day Journal
Document Your Journey!

Living Proverb #1091: "You're a good person. God did a good job in making you, and you've done a good job of making good of what God made!"

Gain 20/20 Vision For The New Decade!
2025 – 365 Day Journal
Document Your Journey!

Living Proverb #1093: "Tremendous success usually requires a larger down-payment of effort."

Gain 20/20 Vision For The New Decade!
2025 – 365 Day Journal
Document Your Journey!

Living Proverb #1095: "Prove yourself to yourself, and let everyone else watch you blossom!"

Gain 20/20 Vision For The New Decade!
2025 – 365 Day Journal
Document Your Journey!

Living Proverb #1096: "If you've been in a process of preparation that seemed to delay, defer, postpone, or hamper the attainment of your desired goal or reward, please be encouraged. God is going to reward you with *double for your trouble!*"

Gain 20/20 Vision For The New Decade!
2025 – 365 Day Journal
Document Your Journey!

Living Proverb #1097: "What do you do with faith? You use it to accomplish the necessary things of life."

Gain 20/20 Vision For The New Decade!
2025 – 365 Day Journal
Document Your Journey!

Living Proverb #1100: "Praise and worship takes you into another realm. It makes you too high for capture by Satan or demon spirits. Praise and worship causes you to transcend the realm of the flesh. You enter the realm of God's holy throne!"

Gain 20/20 Vision For The New Decade!
2025 – 365 Day Journal
Document Your Journey!

Living Proverb #1101: "It takes both the rain and the sunshine to make a life grow. Welcome both as a part of your flourishing future."

Gain 20/20 Vision For The New Decade!
2025 – 365 Day Journal
Document Your Journey!

Living Proverb #1102: "If nothing ever changes, you have to change."

Gain 20/20 Vision For The New Decade!
2025 – 365 Day Journal
Document Your Journey!

Living Proverb #1104: "Life is what you look for. If you look for beauty, life is beautiful. If you look for ugly, life is terrible. The wise person takes a realistic view of both, and decides to be happy and effective in light of the entire picture of life."

Gain 20/20 Vision For The New Decade!
2025 – 365 Day Journal
Document Your Journey!

Living Proverb #1106: "Success starts as an idea, then proceeds to words, and then ends as deeds."

Gain 20/20 Vision For The New Decade!
2025 – 365 Day Journal
Document Your Journey!

Living Proverb #1108: "We must choose life in the face of death. We must choose light in the face of darkness. We always have the right to choose."

Gain 20/20 Vision For The New Decade!
2025 – 365 Day Journal
Document Your Journey!

Living Proverb #1110: "The only cure for a recurring nightmare is a prevailing dream."

Gain 20/20 Vision For The New Decade!
2025 – 365 Day Journal
Document Your Journey!

Living Proverb #1111: "Don't be in such a hurry that you don't take time to get rest. Even NASCAR drivers take pit stops!"

Gain 20/20 Vision For The New Decade!
2025 – 365 Day Journal
Document Your Journey!

Living Proverb #1112: "Excellence speaks for itself, and needs no further explanation."

Gain 20/20 Vision For The New Decade!
2025 – 365 Day Journal
Document Your Journey!

Living Proverb #1113: "You know you have matured in walking with God, when you no longer have to do right by persuasion, or by feeling, but you do right by principle."

Gain 20/20 Vision For The New Decade!
2025 – 365 Day Journal
Document Your Journey!

Living Proverb #1115: "May you always have dishes to wash, and trash to take out, and clothes to wash. In Jesus name, amen."

Gain 20/20 Vision For The New Decade!
2025 – 365 Day Journal
Document Your Journey!

Living Proverb #1116: "Without action there's no satisfaction. Without action there are no results. Without action there's no fulfillment of the promise!"

Gain 20/20 Vision For The New Decade!
2025 – 365 Day Journal
Document Your Journey!

Living Proverb #1117: "If you don't have a clear vision of where you are going, you won't be motivated to get there!"

Gain 20/20 Vision For The New Decade!
2025 – 365 Day Journal
Document Your Journey!

Living Proverb #1118: "Almighty, Jehovah God is the Ancient of Days. There is no problem you could possibly have that He hasn't already seen. He's solved your brand of problem millions of times throughout the ages of the human story. So, relax, and cast all your cares upon Him."

Gain 20/20 Vision For The New Decade!
2025 – 365 Day Journal
Document Your Journey!

Living Proverb #1119: "Diligence is swift insistence on completion of an assigned task in an excellent manner."

Gain 20/20 Vision For The New Decade!
2025 – 365 Day Journal
Document Your Journey!

Living Proverb #1120: "If you receive the images and counsel of the world, it will break your godly focus."

Gain 20/20 Vision For The New Decade!
2025 – 365 Day Journal
Document Your Journey!

Living Proverb #1121: "It's only what you actually do, that will have eventual value. What you fail to do, forfeits the possibility of an eventual treasure."

Gain 20/20 Vision For The New Decade!
2025 – 365 Day Journal
Document Your Journey!

Living Proverb #1122: "Overcome the past with a vision of a brighter future."

Gain 20/20 Vision For The New Decade!
2025 – 365 Day Journal
Document Your Journey!

Living Proverb #1123: "Prayer is the infinite God taking time to socialize with finite mankind."

Gain 20/20 Vision For The New Decade!
2025 – 365 Day Journal
Document Your Journey!

Living Proverb #1124: "In most cases, you won't get nearly as much appreciation as you have the opportunity to give. Therefore, you must learn to give freely, with no strings attached, and love by choice."

Gain 20/20 Vision For The New Decade!
2025 – 365 Day Journal
Document Your Journey!

Living Proverb #1125: "Lasting love is not falling in love. Lasting love is to walk into love with your eyes wide open, accepting one another, and to make a decision. Then, hold to your commitment. It is the true covenant of marriage."

Gain 20/20 Vision For The New Decade!
2025 – 365 Day Journal
Document Your Journey!

Living Proverb #1127: "God's Word doesn't need a co-signer."

Gain 20/20 Vision For The New Decade!
2025 – 365 Day Journal
Document Your Journey!

Living Proverb #1130: "Your associations will determine your location."

Gain 20/20 Vision For The New Decade!
2025 – 365 Day Journal
Document Your Journey!

Living Proverb #1131: "Birds of a feather flock together, and the flock usually ends up in the same place!"

Gain 20/20 Vision For The New Decade!
2025 – 365 Day Journal
Document Your Journey!

Living Proverb #1132: "If you take time to start something, when there seems to be no apparent reward for it, yet you do it with excellence, because it's the right thing to do, there will be an eventual reward."

Gain 20/20 Vision For The New Decade!
2025 – 365 Day Journal
Document Your Journey!

Living Proverb #1133: "Often, how we handle conflict is preparation for promotion."

Gain 20/20 Vision For The New Decade!
2025 – 365 Day Journal
Document Your Journey!

Living Proverb #1134: "Life never changes. God never changes. Life is full of changes. God never changes. God is faithful for all of life's changes."

Gain 20/20 Vision For The New Decade!
2025 – 365 Day Journal
Document Your Journey!

Living Proverb #1135: "The more you give into life the more life gives into you!"

Gain 20/20 Vision For The New Decade!
2025 – 365 Day Journal
Document Your Journey!

Living Proverb #1138: "Once you can think your way out, you can work your way out. Riches start with a state of mind."

70

Gain 20/20 Vision For The New Decade!
2025 – 365 Day Journal
Document Your Journey!

Living Proverb #1139: "Teach your children the fear of the Lord, so they will have boundaries in their decision-making. Then, even if they make a mistake, they will have a guide to go by, and God's mercy to sustain them."

Gain 20/20 Vision For The New Decade!
2025 – 365 Day Journal
Document Your Journey!

Living Proverb #1140: "Whatever you are pursuing, you must allow the heat of your effort to burn out all that is unnecessary, so that all that remains is the gold or silver of your chief definite aim!"

Gain 20/20 Vision For The New Decade!
2025 – 365 Day Journal
Document Your Journey!

Living Proverb #1143: "The key to ongoing success is to do what you know, and to learn what you need to learn."

Gain 20/20 Vision For The New Decade!
2025 – 365 Day Journal
Document Your Journey!

Living Proverb #1144: "Don't be afraid to succeed. You can handle all the requirements and demands of your impending success. You were custom-made for your amazing future!"

Gain 20/20 Vision For The New Decade!
2025 – 365 Day Journal
Document Your Journey!

Living Proverb #1145: "We all start on an equal playing field of time, with 24 hours in a day, 168 hours in a week, and 8760 hours in a year. What will give one person an advantage over another is his or her choice in the use of the time."

Gain 20/20 Vision For The New Decade!
2025 – 365 Day Journal
Document Your Journey!

Living Proverb #1146: "A lion is bold enough to attack an elephant when he's hungry!"

Gain 20/20 Vision For The New Decade!
2025 – 365 Day Journal
Document Your Journey!

Living Proverb #1147: "You can always be promoted to a higher level of doing something, if you're already doing something."

Gain 20/20 Vision For The New Decade!
2025 – 365 Day Journal
Document Your Journey!

Living Proverb #1149: "Be faithful. Be consistent. Be patient. You will never get all of life finished in one day. It's okay!"

Gain 20/20 Vision For The New Decade!
2025 – 365 Day Journal
Document Your Journey!

Living Proverb #1150: "A mind that can imagine is still alive!"

Gain 20/20 Vision For The New Decade!
2025 – 365 Day Journal
Document Your Journey!

Living Proverb #1151: "In life we can't afford mistakes, but we better save up for them, because we all will make them."

Gain 20/20 Vision For The New Decade!
2025 – 365 Day Journal
Document Your Journey!

Living Proverb #1152: "The more focused you become on your God-given purpose will cause you to pay less attention to fickle offenses."

Gain 20/20 Vision For The New Decade!
2025 – 365 Day Journal
Document Your Journey!

Living Proverb #1154: "Rather than to '*boldly go where no man has gone before!*' you should learn what other men and women have already learned, and you will go there too! You can, if you only will!"

Gain 20/20 Vision For The New Decade!
2025 – 365 Day Journal
Document Your Journey!

Living Proverb #1160: "You can't predict the day, so you've got to pray!"

Gain 20/20 Vision For The New Decade!
2025 – 365 Day Journal
Document Your Journey!

Living Proverb #1172: "Just a word of encouragement: Strive to live as long as possible, and make a positive impact on the world in which we live."

Gain 20/20 Vision For The New Decade!
2025 – 365 Day Journal
Document Your Journey!

Living Proverb #1173: "Sometimes it's prayer that helps. Sometimes it's *share* that helps. People need you to talk to God about them, and people need you to talk to them, and share your love, time, and wisdom."

Gain 20/20 Vision For The New Decade!
2025 – 365 Day Journal
Document Your Journey!

Living Proverb #1175: "Dream up to the sky, then come back down to earth, and build your dream up to the heavens."

Gain 20/20 Vision For The New Decade!
2025 – 365 Day Journal
Document Your Journey!

Living Proverb #1180: "After all you've invested, there's nothing left but to succeed. There are no other options, and nowhere else to go. You're over-qualified for anything else but the total successful completion of your destiny."

Gain 20/20 Vision For The New Decade!
2025 – 365 Day Journal
Document Your Journey!

Living Proverb #1181: "Make room! You're in the season of multiplication, abundance, and overflow!"

Gain 20/20 Vision For The New Decade!
2025 – 365 Day Journal
Document Your Journey!

Living Proverb #1191: "When faced with symptoms of sickness, speak to your spirit, because your spirit can revive your body."

Gain 20/20 Vision For The New Decade!
2025 – 365 Day Journal
Document Your Journey!

Living Proverb #1192: "Praise and worship is water and refreshing for the soul!"

Gain 20/20 Vision For The New Decade!
2025 – 365 Day Journal
Document Your Journey!

Living Proverb #1194: "Focus less on overcoming all of your weaknesses and idiosyncrasies, and invest your full amount of energy and focus upon fulfilling God's destiny for your life."

Gain 20/20 Vision For The New Decade!
2025 – 365 Day Journal
Document Your Journey!

Living Proverb #1196: "Fear failure enough to succeed. Don't accept it!"

Gain 20/20 Vision For The New Decade!
2025 – 365 Day Journal
Document Your Journey!

Living Proverb #1200: "You are a specific, specially designed tool to accomplish a specific, predetermined task at this time in the world. Your task was foreseen by the prescient mind of the all-knowing, almighty God."

Gain 20/20 Vision For The New Decade!
2025 – 365 Day Journal
Document Your Journey!

Living Proverb #1201: "God is faithful, even when we don't see a sign of His presence. His Word is true. The just shall live by faith, and not by feelings. God will always come through on His Word. You will come through this season. The Sun is still shining."

Gain 20/20 Vision For The New Decade!
2025 – 365 Day Journal
Document Your Journey!

Living Proverb #1202: "Take a break from the labor of worry today. Cast your cares upon the Lord, for He cares for you!"

Gain 20/20 Vision For The New Decade!
2025 – 365 Day Journal
Document Your Journey!

Living Proverb #1203: "Never take a break from prayer, because your adversary the devil never takes a break in seeking to steal, kill, and destroy in your life."

Gain 20/20 Vision For The New Decade!
2025 – 365 Day Journal
Document Your Journey!

Living Proverb #1204: "Pray while the waters are still, for you can never predict when the next storm will arise."

Gain 20/20 Vision For The New Decade!
2025 – 365 Day Journal
Document Your Journey!

Living Proverb #1205: "If you do what the Word says, you are what the Word says, in spite of what you feel, or how it seems. Also, in spite of who affirms or fails to affirm your identity."

Gain 20/20 Vision For The New Decade!
2025 – 365 Day Journal
Document Your Journey!

Living Proverb #1208: "One simple key to greater success is to do what you do well, and do more of it."

Gain 20/20 Vision For The New Decade!
2025 – 365 Day Journal
Document Your Journey!

Living Proverb #1209: "In life, always be willing to put yourself in the other persons' shoes. Consider how they feel, and consider how they got there, and always know that life has another pair of shoes just like theirs, that are just your size!"

Gain 20/20 Vision For The New Decade!
2025 – 365 Day Journal
Document Your Journey!

Living Proverb #1210: "Front-load the mighty clouds of blessing with the seeds of good works, tithes and offerings, and faithful love. Then when your season of need arises, your harvest of increase will downpour upon your life in refreshing, replenishing rain."

Gain 20/20 Vision For The New Decade!
2025 – 365 Day Journal
Document Your Journey!

Living Proverb #1211: "Jesus has been healing bodies ever since there have been bodies, and there's nobody He can't heal."

Gain 20/20 Vision For The New Decade!
2025 – 365 Day Journal
Document Your Journey!

Living Proverb #1212: "Continually seek wisdom. Continually listen to instruction. Continually incline your heart and ears to insight. Thereby, if your life begins to drift in the wrong direction, you will be alert enough to hear and see the warning signs, and make adjustments."

Gain 20/20 Vision For The New Decade!
2025 – 365 Day Journal
Document Your Journey!

Living Proverb #1215: "Whatever may have been your task today, count your day successful if you are better at the end of the day than at the beginning of it. Even if the day ended unlike you wanted, God's mercy is new for you tomorrow."

Gain 20/20 Vision For The New Decade!
2025 – 365 Day Journal
Document Your Journey!

Living Proverb #1216: "Capture beautiful moments."

Gain 20/20 Vision For The New Decade!
2025 – 365 Day Journal
Document Your Journey!

Living Proverb #1223: "If you show signs that you want to get up, the hand will come!"

Gain 20/20 Vision For The New Decade!
2025 – 365 Day Journal
Document Your Journey!

Living Proverb #1226: "Beauty is in the eye of the beholder. Take time to behold the handiwork of the Lord!"

Gain 20/20 Vision For The New Decade!
2025 – 365 Day Journal
Document Your Journey!

Living Proverb #1227: "Just get it done! Just get it done! Don't be an expert in excuses. Just be an expert in results!"

Gain 20/20 Vision For The New Decade!
2025 – 365 Day Journal
Document Your Journey!

Living Proverb #1228: "People who get paid big money have proven that they can get results."

Gain 20/20 Vision For The New Decade!
2025 – 365 Day Journal
Document Your Journey!

Living Proverb #1229: "Seemingly little things that you do for seemingly little people can make a big difference and speaks great volumes about your character."

Gain 20/20 Vision For The New Decade!
2025 – 365 Day Journal
Document Your Journey!

Living Proverb #1230: "Be thankful today for all God has given you. Jesus is the answer for all the questions of life. How are you going to eat? Jesus is the bread of life. How are you going to rest? Jesus is perfect peace. Jesus is all you need for daily living! Enjoy your day today."

Gain 20/20 Vision For The New Decade!
2025 – 365 Day Journal
Document Your Journey!

Living Proverb #1232: "One person changed can change the world."

Gain 20/20 Vision For The New Decade!
2025 – 365 Day Journal
Document Your Journey!

Living Proverb #1233: "Every step forward is a step in the right direction."

Gain 20/20 Vision For The New Decade!
2025 – 365 Day Journal
Document Your Journey!

Living Proverb #1234: "If you truly recognize your value, you can make hundreds of thousands of dollars in your profession, but you can make millions of dollars in your gifts and talents."

Gain 20/20 Vision For The New Decade!
2025 – 365 Day Journal
Document Your Journey!

Living Proverb #1237: "When you know who you are, no one can stop the force of who you are, and the force of who you are will change your whole situation."

Gain 20/20 Vision For The New Decade!
2025 – 365 Day Journal
Document Your Journey!

Living Proverb #1601: "In once-in-a-lifetime opportunities, you have to use your *"mind-biscuit"* to *sop-up* all of the gravy off of the plate. Tomorrow is not promised. If you are in school, college, or a special training opportunity, be sure to make the most of it."

Gain 20/20 Vision For The New Decade!
2025 – 365 Day Journal
Document Your Journey!

Living Proverb #1610: "God is not new at causing people to succeed. What He has done for others, He will do for you. All you have to do is obey His principles of faith, wisdom, diligence, and perseverance."

Gain 20/20 Vision For The New Decade!
2025 – 365 Day Journal
Document Your Journey!

Living Proverb #1611: "Whatever may be your sorrow, pain, failure, or disappointment, know that God is your source of redemption, joy, and lifelong victory. God is for you; God is with you; and God is in you. Lay down your pain for the joy of the Lord."

Gain 20/20 Vision For The New Decade!
2025 – 365 Day Journal
Document Your Journey!

Living Proverb #1614: "Be who you are, and people will see who you are, and you won't have to say who you are. You don't have to brag. Let your *works* speak louder than your words."

Gain 20/20 Vision For The New Decade!
2025 – 365 Day Journal
Document Your Journey!

Living Proverb #1617: "In relationships, sometimes it's not your words that are needed. It's your listening ear. Sometimes just through your time and understanding, people can *untangle themselves*."

Gain 20/20 Vision For The New Decade!
2025 – 365 Day Journal
Document Your Journey!

Living Proverb #1618: "Success is not a random miracle. Success is a sure process. If you follow success principles, which are available to all, you will succeed. Success is the norm, and not the exception. If we follow the sure patterns that have been recorded, we will succeed."

Gain 20/20 Vision For The New Decade!
2025 – 365 Day Journal
Document Your Journey!

Living Proverb #1619: "Allow the light of God to fully shine through you this week. Show your difference. Show your love. Show your brilliance. Shine for Jesus. You are the light of the world."

Gain 20/20 Vision For The New Decade!
2025 – 365 Day Journal
Document Your Journey!

Living Proverb #1620: "You may have a lot of things to be concerned about, but pray. Jesus is in control. So, you have nothing to worry about."

Gain 20/20 Vision For The New Decade!
2025 – 365 Day Journal
Document Your Journey!

Living Proverb #1621: "Often, the greatest friendship is correction."

Gain 20/20 Vision For The New Decade!
2025 – 365 Day Journal
Document Your Journey!

Living Proverb #1622: "Truly great people are *gracious* people."

Gain 20/20 Vision For The New Decade!
2025 – 365 Day Journal
Document Your Journey!

Living Proverb #1623: "There's rarely any drawback to being early. But, there's typically always a negative stigma to being late. Particularly, when you're cooperating with busy, diligent people. There's no perfection. Yet, everyone should be striving for the same standard."

Gain 20/20 Vision For The New Decade!
2025 – 365 Day Journal
Document Your Journey!

Living Proverb #1624: "Some days *you* make happen. Some days *make themselves happen*. When you're led by the Holy Spirit your spirit can lead you faster than your mind can conceive. Even when you can't control all of the details or circumstances, you made progress."

Gain 20/20 Vision For The New Decade!
2025 – 365 Day Journal
Document Your Journey!

Living Proverb #1625: "You don't need a sign. You need an assignment."

Gain 20/20 Vision For The New Decade!
2025 – 365 Day Journal
Document Your Journey!

Living Proverb #1629: "Don't focus so much on waiting on your blessing to come toward you. Rather, focus on doing what's required so that you are moving toward your blessing. Then, and only then, is your blessing *guaranteed*!"

Gain 20/20 Vision For The New Decade!
2025 – 365 Day Journal
Document Your Journey!

Living Proverb #1630: "The evident sign of genius is *productivity*."

Gain 20/20 Vision For The New Decade!
2025 – 365 Day Journal
Document Your Journey!

Living Proverb #1631: "Success is a good *investment*. Once you get started, success is cumulative like *compound interest*."

Gain 20/20 Vision For The New Decade!
2025 – 365 Day Journal
Document Your Journey!

Living Proverb #1632: "No matter what you're facing today, know that the Lord is working on your behalf! He loves you!"

Gain 20/20 Vision For The New Decade!
2025 – 365 Day Journal
Document Your Journey!

Living Proverb #1633: "Praying without ceasing doesn't take a longtime. It just takes *oftentimes*."

Gain 20/20 Vision For The New Decade!
2025 – 365 Day Journal
Document Your Journey!

Living Proverb #1635: "You're young enough for your dreams. You're strong enough for your dreams. You know enough to obtain your dreams. And you're well able to *possess your land*!"

Gain 20/20 Vision For The New Decade!
2025 – 365 Day Journal
Document Your Journey!

Living Proverb #1636: "Anytime is a good time to take a praise break unto God for all of His goodness, mercy, and loving-kindness to you and your family! Praise Him! It will make you feel better! He deserves it. It's all about Him after all!"

Gain 20/20 Vision For The New Decade!
2025 – 365 Day Journal
Document Your Journey!

Living Proverb #1646: "Keep sowing good seed, because during harvest time, only the seed you've actually sown will come up!"

Gain 20/20 Vision For The New Decade!
2025 – 365 Day Journal
Document Your Journey!

Living Proverb #1647: "The greatest lesson that you can learn in life is the ability to think for yourself."

Gain 20/20 Vision For The New Decade!
2025 – 365 Day Journal
Document Your Journey!

Living Proverb #1649: "In the game of life, if you want to play, you had better pray!"

Gain 20/20 Vision For The New Decade!
2025 – 365 Day Journal
Document Your Journey!

Living Proverb #1652: "There's no better time to solve a problem than when it is a problem, so that it won't continue to be a problem."

Gain 20/20 Vision For The New Decade!
2025 – 365 Day Journal
Document Your Journey!

Living Proverb #1653: "You don't have to be hateful to be truthful, but, you have to be truthful to be *free*."

Gain 20/20 Vision For The New Decade!
2025 – 365 Day Journal
Document Your Journey!

Living Proverb #1654: "If you want to please God, just start moving in the direction. He knows your heart and He's not looking for perfection. Start taking steps, step-by-step, and God will get you there."

Gain 20/20 Vision For The New Decade!
2025 – 365 Day Journal
Document Your Journey!

Living Proverb #1655: "If you respect money, money will respect you. If you disrespect money, money will leave you. Respecting money means to be watchful over it. Tend to it, take care of it, and it will stay with you. If you disrespect it, it will fly away like an eagle toward the heavens."

Gain 20/20 Vision For The New Decade!
2025 – 365 Day Journal
Document Your Journey!

Living Proverb #1659: "If you show a little hunger, wisdom will come searching for you. Wisdom is for the wise: those wise enough to know that they need it."

Gain 20/20 Vision For The New Decade!
2025 – 365 Day Journal
Document Your Journey!

Living Proverb #1661: "If you will outlast the devil, the devil will lose, because you've already won. It is the *"good fight of faith"*, because you have already won. Yet, you must resist the devil, and he will flee from you."

Gain 20/20 Vision For The New Decade!
2025 – 365 Day Journal
Document Your Journey!

Living Proverb #1662: "No matter what you may be facing today, no matter your circumstances, leave your care in the hand of the Lord, for He cares for you. He will make it alright. He will work it out for your good. In that place of trust, you can truly say, 'It Is Well With My Soul.'"

Gain 20/20 Vision For The New Decade!
2025 – 365 Day Journal
Document Your Journey!

Living Proverb #1663: "Wisdom is not knowledge. Wisdom is developed or given. Knowledge must be *pursued*. Wise is the person who discerns that he or she needs more knowledge, and has the discipline to get it, and to use it to achieve the desired purposes."

Gain 20/20 Vision For The New Decade!
2025 – 365 Day Journal
Document Your Journey!

Living Proverb #1664: "In financial decisions, the bottom line is the bottom line. Decide based on the bottom line. If taking from your bottom line to give to someone else's bottom line causes your bottom line to grow, then do it. Always decide based on the bottom line."

Gain 20/20 Vision For The New Decade!
2025 – 365 Day Journal
Document Your Journey!

Living Proverb #1666: "The future is in your hands. So, manage it well. What you do today will greatly impact tomorrow's outcomes."

Gain 20/20 Vision For The New Decade!
2025 – 365 Day Journal
Document Your Journey!

Living Proverb #1667: "One speaker asked the question, 'Would you rather have 20 half carat diamonds, or one 10 carat diamond?' I say, 'I'll take both' Leave no value on the table. Everything has value when properly marketed."

Gain 20/20 Vision For The New Decade!
2025 – 365 Day Journal
Document Your Journey!

Living Proverb #1668: "Marketing makes the revenue wheel go round!"

Gain 20/20 Vision For The New Decade!
2025 – 365 Day Journal
Document Your Journey!

Living Proverb #1670: "If you set big goals, you'll accomplish big things. If you set small goals, you'll accomplish small things. If you set no goals, you'll accomplish *nothing*."

Gain 20/20 Vision For The New Decade!
2025 – 365 Day Journal
Document Your Journey!

Living Proverb #1671: "People with purpose make the best students. You don't have to give them a reason to stay motivated, focused, and passionate."

Gain 20/20 Vision For The New Decade!
2025 – 365 Day Journal
Document Your Journey!

Living Proverb #1672: "I declare that a mighty wave of success has been rolling and rolling and rolling, and moving forward underneath the surface of your life, and it's about to break through the surface like a mighty wave of a *blessing tsunami*!"

Gain 20/20 Vision For The New Decade!
2025 – 365 Day Journal
Document Your Journey!

Living Proverb #1673: "The sign of a true entrepreneur is the ability to create great things out of limited resources."

Gain 20/20 Vision For The New Decade!
2025 – 365 Day Journal
Document Your Journey!

Living Proverb #1674: "The key to maintaining our peace is to learn to live an uncomplicated life in the midst of a very complicated world. Jesus is the key to peace. Jesus is the answer for the world today."

Gain 20/20 Vision For The New Decade!
2025 – 365 Day Journal
Document Your Journey!

Living Proverb #1675: "You must win the *inner* battle before you can win the outer battle."

Gain 20/20 Vision For The New Decade!
2025 – 365 Day Journal
Document Your Journey!

Living Proverb #1676: "If you would like a fresh start to your mental day, take time to read five or ten chapters of one of the four gospels, Matthew, Mark, Luke, or John. Read it aloud, so that your spirit and mind will hear you saying it. You will find it to be refreshing."

Gain 20/20 Vision For The New Decade!
2025 – 365 Day Journal
Document Your Journey!

Living Proverb #1680: "One word from God can open your eyes from being *'future-blind'* and almost hopeless, to being passionately focused and hopeful for your future."

Gain 20/20 Vision For The New Decade!
2025 – 365 Day Journal
Document Your Journey!

Living Proverb #1682: "As a destiny person, your destiny is complete as soon as you make a decision to pursue it. You're not creating the destiny. You just decided to *pursue* it, and when you decided, it is done. All you must do is take the necessary steps. '*It is finished.*'"

Gain 20/20 Vision For The New Decade!
2025 – 365 Day Journal
Document Your Journey!

Living Proverb #1683: "If your money doesn't have a specific place to go, it will go."

Gain 20/20 Vision For The New Decade!
2025 – 365 Day Journal
Document Your Journey!

Living Proverb #1684: "Ask people nicely, and they will do more for you so much easier."

Gain 20/20 Vision For The New Decade!
2025 – 365 Day Journal
Document Your Journey!

Living Proverb #1685: "Once you reach a certain level of maturity, God expects you to rule yourself. He expects you to rule your own time, eating habits, work habits, and all areas of your life. That takes courage and commitment. However, you were born to rule and reign."

Gain 20/20 Vision For The New Decade!
2025 – 365 Day Journal
Document Your Journey!

Living Proverb #1689: "*Opportunity* is a walking Man. If you don't stop Him to sit down and have dinner, and to hear Him speak, He will keep walking on by."

Gain 20/20 Vision For The New Decade!
2025 – 365 Day Journal
Document Your Journey!

Living Proverb #1691: "God prepares you for life. If you keep on walking by faith, you'll be prepared for the *next leg* of the race."

Gain 20/20 Vision For The New Decade!
2025 – 365 Day Journal
Document Your Journey!

Living Proverb #1692: "Go with the *flow of favor* in life, because you don't know what the future will hold. You will need it. Go with the flow of favor. Do the right thing when it's the right time, and you will have the right harvest at the right time."

Gain 20/20 Vision For The New Decade!
2025 – 365 Day Journal
Document Your Journey!

Living Proverb #1694: "The greatest thing that you can do for your family is to be successful. Abraham had to leave his family to go and succeed. Isaac succeeded. Jacob went and succeeded. The greatest thing that you can do for your family is to be successful."

Gain 20/20 Vision For The New Decade!
2025 – 365 Day Journal
Document Your Journey!

Living Proverb #1700: "Regarding doing the work of God, prepare like it all depended on you, but seek God like it all depended on Him."

Gain 20/20 Vision For The New Decade!
2025 – 365 Day Journal
Document Your Journey!

Living Proverb #1701: "You may feel like you need to make more money, but if you focus on making more progress, you will make more money."

Gain 20/20 Vision For The New Decade!
2025 – 365 Day Journal
Document Your Journey!

Living Proverb #1705: "You will always win a battle if you keep your peace."

Gain 20/20 Vision For The New Decade!
2025 – 365 Day Journal
Document Your Journey!

Living Proverb #1706: "Keep your head up. Walk like a king. Stay up and never slide down. Be the victor and not the victim. And never let anybody put you on the *back of the bus*!"

Gain 20/20 Vision For The New Decade!
2025 – 365 Day Journal
Document Your Journey!

Living Proverb #1707: "Respect for yourself and others will make for a respectable relationship."

Gain 20/20 Vision For The New Decade!
2025 – 365 Day Journal
Document Your Journey!

Living Proverb #1708: "Here's a lesson: Never miss an opportunity to be a blessing to others, even when it takes courage to say something or to do something. Always choose to be a blessing to others."

Gain 20/20 Vision For The New Decade!
2025 – 365 Day Journal
Document Your Journey!

Living Proverb #1709: "Faith comes by hearing. Faith is the ability to take action. If you have not been taking enough action in life, you must take time to build up your faith, by listening to things that can help build up your motivation to take action. Faith comes by hearing."

Gain 20/20 Vision For The New Decade!
2025 – 365 Day Journal
Document Your Journey!

Living Proverb #1712: "Creation is the first phase of profit. You can always sell something that you have. You can't sell something that you don't have. Creation is the first phase of profit."

Gain 20/20 Vision For The New Decade!
2025 – 365 Day Journal
Document Your Journey!

Living Proverb #1713: "Nobody is concerned about doing what you need to do, but you. If you don't do it, it won't get done. If you don't run your race, it won't be run. Nobody is concerned about you, and what you need to do, but you."

Gain 20/20 Vision For The New Decade!
2025 – 365 Day Journal
Document Your Journey!

Living Proverb #1714: "Do big things and you will become larger. Do even more big things, and you will become larger even *faster*."

Gain 20/20 Vision For The New Decade!
2025 – 365 Day Journal
Document Your Journey!

Living Proverb #1715: "Knowledge comes from learning and study. Growing comes from doing."

Gain 20/20 Vision For The New Decade!
2025 – 365 Day Journal
Document Your Journey!

Living Proverb #1716: "When life becomes confusing, pray in the Holy Ghost. Pray out the answers to those mysteries."

Gain 20/20 Vision For The New Decade!
2025 – 365 Day Journal
Document Your Journey!

Living Proverb #1718: "Don't listen to *'loser talk'*, even if it's coming from a winner. Rather, pay attention to what the winner is doing and follow their *example*, and you'll become a winner too."

Gain 20/20 Vision For The New Decade!
2025 – 365 Day Journal
Document Your Journey!

Living Proverb #1719: "Regarding sales, continue to create excellence, and be productive, rather than overly focusing on the sales process. You can always sell something that you have, but you can't sell something that you don't have. Therefore, focus on being productive and excellent."

Gain 20/20 Vision For The New Decade!
2025 – 365 Day Journal
Document Your Journey!

Living Proverb #1720: "Close the circle of productivity with profit."

Gain 20/20 Vision For The New Decade!
2025 – 365 Day Journal
Document Your Journey!

Living Proverb #1721: "Favor *plus* labor equals success."

Gain 20/20 Vision For The New Decade!
2025 – 365 Day Journal
Document Your Journey!

Living Proverb #1722: "Success may be slow, but success is sure, if you keep working on the right things in the right way overtime. Success may be slow, but success is sure."

Gain 20/20 Vision For The New Decade!
2025 – 365 Day Journal
Document Your Journey!

Living Proverb #1723: "Life takes faith and trust. It takes faith to go forward and trust to be patient in the process."

Gain 20/20 Vision For The New Decade!
2025 – 365 Day Journal
Document Your Journey!

Living Proverb #1724: "May you demonstrate the style of a victor, and not a victim: a winner and not a whiner. Greater is He who is in you, than he that is in the world. And if God be for you, who can be against you?"

Gain 20/20 Vision For The New Decade!
2025 – 365 Day Journal
Document Your Journey!

Living Proverb #1725: "A life built upon truth *appreciates* in value over time. A life built upon falsehood declines and *depreciates* in value over time."

Gain 20/20 Vision For The New Decade!
2025 – 365 Day Journal
Document Your Journey!

Living Proverb #1726: "Patience and planning are the keys to financial freedom. Impatience and impulsiveness are the keys to continued poverty."

Gain 20/20 Vision For The New Decade!
2025 – 365 Day Journal
Document Your Journey!

Living Proverb #1727: "There are many thoughts that may go through your mind about what you had to do today, but what you actually had to do, you did it. Each day must stand on its on."

Gain 20/20 Vision For The New Decade!
2025 – 365 Day Journal
Document Your Journey!

Living Proverb #1728: "Become comfortable with being great. Come out of your comfort zone. Even a turtle will stick its neck out when it becomes comfortable. If you do, you may be surprised and realize that you are a *giraffe*!"

Gain 20/20 Vision For The New Decade!
2025 – 365 Day Journal
Document Your Journey!

Living Proverb #1729: "Take time to meditate and confess God's Word over every area of your life. Allow God's Word to pierce through the darkness. Do not let your vision of the future be suffocated by circumstances. Rather, pierce through the darkness with God's Word."

Gain 20/20 Vision For The New Decade!
2025 – 365 Day Journal
Document Your Journey!

Living Proverb #1730: "The eyes are the windows to the soul. Be careful of what you allow into the house. It could be darkness, or it could be light. One will blind your purpose. The other will enlighten your way. Be careful of what you allow into the house."

Gain 20/20 Vision For The New Decade!
2025 – 365 Day Journal
Document Your Journey!

Living Proverb #1731: "The '*good fight of faith*' that you have been in is preparation for the next level. God can't let you be a wimp when you're destined to become '*the head and not the tail.*' You've got to be tough to be '*large and in charge!*'"

Gain 20/20 Vision For The New Decade!
2025 – 365 Day Journal
Document Your Journey!

Living Proverb #1732: "If you focus on saving money, you will save a lot of money. If you focus on spending money, you will spend a lot of money. Focus is the key to financial freedom or financial poverty."

Gain 20/20 Vision For The New Decade!
2025 – 365 Day Journal
Document Your Journey!

Living Proverb #1733: "Average people will often try to judge above average people in order to bring them down to their level."

Gain 20/20 Vision For The New Decade!
2025 – 365 Day Journal
Document Your Journey!

Living Proverb #1734: "People who *get it done* like to work with people who get it done."

Gain 20/20 Vision For The New Decade!
2025 – 365 Day Journal
Document Your Journey!

Living Proverb #1736: "Giving says more about the giver than it does about the receiver."

Gain 20/20 Vision For The New Decade!
2025 – 365 Day Journal
Document Your Journey!

Living Proverb #1737: "Both fear and faith are alternate states of reality. Take time to dwell in the alternate state of faith, and you will change your reality. Avoid fear, because it is not a place that you want to be in. Choose faith and you will change your reality."

Gain 20/20 Vision For The New Decade!
2025 – 365 Day Journal
Document Your Journey!

Living Proverb #1738: "When it's time for your blessing, God can compress time to get it to you. Time is not a factor when it's time for your blessing. When you're ready, God will get you there."

Gain 20/20 Vision For The New Decade!
2025 – 365 Day Journal
Document Your Journey!

Living Proverb #1741: "There's no conundrum or challenge in your life that someone else hasn't faced in some form or fashion before you. The answer is inside of the Bible. It may be in another book, another person, or inside of your spirit. You can draw it out through prayer."

Gain 20/20 Vision For The New Decade!
2025 – 365 Day Journal
Document Your Journey!

Living Proverb #1744: "God has enabled you. God has made you able. God has provided you with the means, opportunity, power, and authority to be successful. He's made it possible. Step out in faith. Use what you have, and success is guaranteed!"

Gain 20/20 Vision For The New Decade!
2025 – 365 Day Journal
Document Your Journey!

Living Proverb #1748: "Exercise, healthy food, and rest help the body and mind deal with stress, so that you can do your best. It helps you recalibrate. It balances the chemicals in the body and brain. If you want to do your best, be sure to exercise, eat right, and get your rest."

Gain 20/20 Vision For The New Decade!
2025 – 365 Day Journal
Document Your Journey!

Living Proverb #1753: "You must do what's required to obtain what's desired. What's required usually is much more than what you at first anticipated."

Gain 20/20 Vision For The New Decade!
2025 – 365 Day Journal
Document Your Journey!

Living Proverb #1754: "You've lost perspective when you start to throw away good food just because you're full. You've lost perspective when you start to throw away good people, just because you're tired of them."

Gain 20/20 Vision For The New Decade!
2025 – 365 Day Journal
Document Your Journey!

Living Proverb #1755: "Always be thinking problem prevention, and you'll avoid a lot of problems."

Gain 20/20 Vision For The New Decade!
2025 – 365 Day Journal
Document Your Journey!

Living Proverb #1756: "The beginning of healthy relationships is at the casting out of fear."

Gain 20/20 Vision For The New Decade!
2025 – 365 Day Journal
Document Your Journey!

Living Proverb #1759: "Life is like a close race. The person who *leans in* will win. Lean in! Put your heart into the race!"

Gain 20/20 Vision For The New Decade!
2025 – 365 Day Journal
Document Your Journey!

Living Proverb #1760: "Some things are better unsaid."

Gain 20/20 Vision For The New Decade!
2025 – 365 Day Journal
Document Your Journey!

Living Proverb #1761: "A good friend is not afraid to tell you the truth."

Gain 20/20 Vision For The New Decade!
2025 – 365 Day Journal
Document Your Journey!

Living Proverb #1762: "Give honor to whom honor is due. Honor is an *earned asset* that has lasting value. Once you have done what's necessary to attain it, you must do all within your power to maintain it. Honor is a precious *gift*."

Gain 20/20 Vision For The New Decade!
2025 – 365 Day Journal
Document Your Journey!

Living Proverb #1763: "What's done in the dark will eventually come to the light."

Gain 20/20 Vision For The New Decade!
2025 – 365 Day Journal
Document Your Journey!

Living Proverb #1764: "Success is achievable. You can obtain it if you train for it. You must prepare for success. You must run the race to win. You must keep your eyes on the prize, and lay aside everything that hinders you in the race. Success is achievable. You were born to win."

Gain 20/20 Vision For The New Decade!
2025 – 365 Day Journal
Document Your Journey!

Living Proverb #1765: "Sometimes it's more glory for people to see you struggle and overcome, than to be able to act like you have no problems and fake people out. There's glory in your struggles."

Gain 20/20 Vision For The New Decade!
2025 – 365 Day Journal
Document Your Journey!

Living Proverb #1766: "The best meals have plenty of flavor without being overly filling. The best conversations have plenty of meaning without an overuse of words."

Gain 20/20 Vision For The New Decade!
2025 – 365 Day Journal
Document Your Journey!

Living Proverb #1767: "As you take care of others, be sure to take care of you, because no one will take care of you, like you're supposed to take care of you."

Gain 20/20 Vision For The New Decade!
2025 – 365 Day Journal
Document Your Journey!

Living Proverb #1769: "You are an optimum, excellent, superior, outstanding, godly, exceptional person. You fulfill God's highest ideals. You're pleasing to God. He loves you very much. He wishes above all things that you prosper, be in health, even as your soul prospers."

Gain 20/20 Vision For The New Decade!
2025 – 365 Day Journal
Document Your Journey!

Living Proverb #1770: "Listen to the customers, rather than listening to the experts. The customers are the experts."

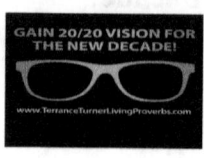

Gain 20/20 Vision For The New Decade!
2025 – 365 Day Journal
Document Your Journey!

Living Proverb #1773: "In some circles, a new idea will be celebrated and exalted as very valuable or priceless or worth $1 million or more. In other circles, that same new idea will be passed by as almost worthless. Determination of value is based on the minds it's introduced to."

Gain 20/20 Vision For The New Decade!
2025 – 365 Day Journal
Document Your Journey!

Living Proverb #1775: "Take precautions, and thus, save repairs."

Gain 20/20 Vision For The New Decade!
2025 – 365 Day Journal
Document Your Journey!

Living Proverb #1776: "The only way to heal the other person is to heal you. Never hate another. Rather, love yourself. Thus, freeing you from the hatred or manipulation of another person."

Gain 20/20 Vision For The New Decade!
2025 – 365 Day Journal
Document Your Journey!

Living Proverb #1778: "You should seek the blessing that God promises to every person who worships and reverences Him. That is, to profit from the labor of your own hands, to be happy in life, to have a successful, fruitful family life, and to live a long, healthy life."

Gain 20/20 Vision For The New Decade!
2025 – 365 Day Journal
Document Your Journey!

Living Proverb #1779: "God's grace can help you deal with the real, and cause your life to go from being less than ideal to becoming fulfilled."

Gain 20/20 Vision For The New Decade!
2025 – 365 Day Journal
Document Your Journey!

Living Proverb #1780: "Love is unfeigned commitment for an indefinite period of time. The commitment involves kindness, care, and the intentional betterment of the other person. There are no ulterior motives in addition to the choice and commitment to love."

Gain 20/20 Vision For The New Decade!
2025 – 365 Day Journal
Document Your Journey!

Living Proverb #1784: "Hold your peace, and don't let anyone steal it. Overcome evil with good. Overcome disorder with order. Overcome intimidation with calm confidence. Overcome blame with righteousness. Hold your peace, and don't let anyone steal it."

Gain 20/20 Vision For The New Decade!
2025 – 365 Day Journal
Document Your Journey!

Living Proverb #1785: "If you ask anybody that is *somebody* how they became somebody, they will tell you that it took a lot of hard, smart work."

Gain 20/20 Vision For The New Decade!
2025 – 365 Day Journal
Document Your Journey!

Living Proverb #1788: "What gets measured can be managed. Whether its's time, money, calories, steps, etc. What gets measured can be managed."

Gain 20/20 Vision For The New Decade!
2025 – 365 Day Journal
Document Your Journey!

Living Proverb #1789: "Life can be eventful. Handle it with prayer."

Gain 20/20 Vision For The New Decade!
2025 – 365 Day Journal
Document Your Journey!

Living Proverb #1790: "God always responds to faith. Prosperity always responds to order. You need faith and order to create and maintain prosperity."

Gain 20/20 Vision For The New Decade!
2025 – 365 Day Journal
Document Your Journey!

Living Proverb #1791: "Whatever you're facing in this moment, God has grace for you. Grace is God's ability to do for you, in you, or through you, what you don't have the ability to do in your own strength. It is God's *super* on your natural. Grace will give you supernatural results."

Gain 20/20 Vision For The New Decade!
2025 – 365 Day Journal
Document Your Journey!

Living Proverb #1792: "The first stage of profit is *learning*."

Gain 20/20 Vision For The New Decade!
2025 – 365 Day Journal
Document Your Journey!

Living Proverb #1793: "The longer you wait the less gets accomplished. You've got to stay on the run, to get the job done."

~~Pastor Avis Turner, MD

Gain 20/20 Vision For The New Decade!
2025 – 365 Day Journal
Document Your Journey!

Living Proverb #1794: "Singing praise and worship music releases *endorphins* and *angels* on your behalf. Take time to sing praise and worship. You will be blessed and protected."

Gain 20/20 Vision For The New Decade!
2025 – 365 Day Journal
Document Your Journey!

Living Proverb #1795: "There's rarely any drawback to keeping your mouth shut."

Gain 20/20 Vision For The New Decade!
2025 – 365 Day Journal
Document Your Journey!

Living Proverb #1796: "A lot of times you can get more answers by being quiet than you can by talking."

Gain 20/20 Vision For The New Decade!
2025 – 365 Day Journal
Document Your Journey!

Living Proverb #1797: "Life is short. You've got to be patient."

Gain 20/20 Vision For The New Decade!
2025 – 365 Day Journal
Document Your Journey!

Living Proverb #1798: "Life goes on. You should too!"

Gain 20/20 Vision For The New Decade!
2025 – 365 Day Journal
Document Your Journey!

Living Proverb #1799: "Never get so sophisticated that you can't say, 'Thank You Jesus!'"

Gain 20/20 Vision For The New Decade!
2025 – 365 Day Journal
Document Your Journey!

Living Proverb #1800: "Life happens. You must be able to *pivot*."

Gain 20/20 Vision For The New Decade!
2025 – 365 Day Journal
Document Your Journey!

Living Proverb #1801: "Prior to every meeting, always remember that every conversation was *proceeded* by a conversation. Therefore, never be careless in your conversations."

Gain 20/20 Vision For The New Decade!
2025 – 365 Day Journal
Document Your Journey!

Living Proverb #1802: "When you have a destiny to accomplish, God is working harder than you are to make sure it comes to pass. However, you still have to work with God."

Gain 20/20 Vision For The New Decade!
2025 – 365 Day Journal
Document Your Journey!

Living Proverb #1804: "There's more than one way of teaching. If you're a good student, then you are able to adjust your learning capacity to the specific lessons of life."

Gain 20/20 Vision For The New Decade!
2025 – 365 Day Journal
Document Your Journey!

Living Proverb #1805: "Have a plan, yet, be open to the possibilities of God."

Gain 20/20 Vision For The New Decade!
2025 – 365 Day Journal
Document Your Journey!

Living Proverb #1806: "Keep on producing with excellence. Make your *own* name. You won't need anyone else's name."

Gain 20/20 Vision For The New Decade!
2025 – 365 Day Journal
Document Your Journey!

Living Proverb #1807: "When people can *make* you, then, people can *break* you. Therefore, keep your eyes upon Jesus. Do what God has called you to do. Pay the price to become qualified. Then, make your *own* luck."

Gain 20/20 Vision For The New Decade!
2025 – 365 Day Journal
Document Your Journey!

Living Proverb #1808: "When you know your own value, you won't *cheapen* your asking price."

Gain 20/20 Vision For The New Decade!
2025 – 365 Day Journal
Document Your Journey!

Living Proverb #1809: "Don't spend your time tending to someone else's business. Rather, spend your time tending to your own business, because, that's what's going to *pay* you."

Gain 20/20 Vision For The New Decade!
2025 – 365 Day Journal
Document Your Journey!

Living Proverb #1810: "Regarding creating a future for your family, go ahead! Go ahead! Somebody has to go ahead in order to create a prosperous posterity for your family. Don't be afraid to be the first. Don't be afraid to go ahead! Go ahead! Create a future for your family."

Gain 20/20 Vision For The New Decade!
2025 – 365 Day Journal
Document Your Journey!

Living Proverb #1811: "We are saved by grace, through faith, and not by works, lest anyone should boast. Therefore, if you're saved by grace, and do not do any good works, you can still be saved. However, you won't be satisfied. Satisfaction come from accomplishing great deeds."

Gain 20/20 Vision For The New Decade!
2025 – 365 Day Journal
Document Your Journey!

Living Proverb #1813: "Just do the right thing, and don't decide what you are going to do based on popular opinion. You'll be happier in the end."

Gain 20/20 Vision For The New Decade!
2025 – 365 Day Journal
Document Your Journey!

Living Proverb #1814: "You can't hide quality, and you can't really fake it. You must develop it. Be the best at what God made you to do, and be the best you that God made you to be, by continual self-development."

Gain 20/20 Vision For The New Decade!
2025 – 365 Day Journal
Document Your Journey!

Living Proverb #1815: "People who are not doing anything have nothing better to do than to talk about people who are doing something. Therefore, the best thing for people who are doing something to do is to ignore the talk of those who are not doing anything."

Gain 20/20 Vision For The New Decade!
2025 – 365 Day Journal
Document Your Journey!

Living Proverb #1816: "If Christians would pray several times a day, we would be less carnal, more spiritual, and more successful. As we stay in continual fellowship with Jehovah, the God of the universe, we will act, talk, and look more like Him."

Gain 20/20 Vision For The New Decade!
2025 – 365 Day Journal
Document Your Journey!

Living Proverb #1818: "When you know your ways please the Lord, you can have soul satisfaction! You know you're doing alright. Nothing else besides has very much consequence. You please the Lord by obeying His principles in the Bible."

Gain 20/20 Vision For The New Decade!
2025 – 365 Day Journal
Document Your Journey!

Living Proverb #1819: "If we will restrict our diets while we are free to choose, we won't be forced to restrict our diets."

Gain 20/20 Vision For The New Decade!
2025 – 365 Day Journal
Document Your Journey!

Living Proverb #1820: "We often miss potential miracles, because we fail to notice and value the flowers that grow in between the cracks of time. Every miracle may not happen on your schedule. However, you must be alert enough to capture the potential beauty when it arises."

Gain 20/20 Vision For The New Decade!
2025 – 365 Day Journal
Document Your Journey!

Living Proverb #1821: "In life, you have to take opportunities! They're not just handed to you. You must take opportunities for rest, recreation, idea creation, advancement, etc. You must take opportunities, because, in most cases, they will not just be handed to you."

Gain 20/20 Vision For The New Decade!
2025 – 365 Day Journal
Document Your Journey!

Living Proverb #1822: "In regard to the will of God, if you haven't succeeded, its's because you haven't done your best. If you do your best, you'll be a success. Either, there's a lack of knowledge or a lack of action upon the knowledge that you have. You were born to succeed."

Gain 20/20 Vision For The New Decade!
2025 – 365 Day Journal
Document Your Journey!

Living Proverb #1823: "Don't settle for defeat! Keep striving to do your best, in spite of setbacks or opposition! There's more in you than you know! Don't settle for defeat! Keep striving for the best! Stay in the race!."

Gain 20/20 Vision For The New Decade!
2025 – 365 Day Journal
Document Your Journey!

Living Proverb #1824: "Challenges make champions better!"

Gain 20/20 Vision For The New Decade!
2025 – 365 Day Journal
Document Your Journey!

Living Proverb #1825: "God doesn't bring His Word down to our performance. He brings His grace down to our performance, in order to help us come up to the standards of His Word. However, He never lowers the standard of His Word. He exalts His Word above His name."

Gain 20/20 Vision For The New Decade!
2025 – 365 Day Journal
Document Your Journey!

Living Proverb #1826: "Regarding success, it's about execution. And, it's not over until the *cash register sings!*"

Gain 20/20 Vision For The New Decade!
2025 – 365 Day Journal
Document Your Journey!

Living Proverb #1827: "Be the CEO of your own life. Set your own goals. Set your own deadlines. Then, do what's necessary to accomplish them. Be accountable to yourself, and keep your own counsel. Be your own boss."

Gain 20/20 Vision For The New Decade!
2025 – 365 Day Journal
Document Your Journey!

Living Proverb #1828: "Jump-start your day with a song of praise! Recognize God as the 'Author' of your new day! Give Him thanksgiving for blessing you in all your ways. Jump-start each day with a song of praise! God deserves it, and you will feel better."

Gain 20/20 Vision For The New Decade!
2025 – 365 Day Journal
Document Your Journey!

Living Proverb #1832: "Learn a lesson from the birds: talk to and praise God early in the morning."

Gain 20/20 Vision For The New Decade!
2025 – 365 Day Journal
Document Your Journey!

Living Proverb #1834: "Most people are full of excuses today, and full of *regrets* tomorrow. Take action today, and you'll be happier tomorrow."

Gain 20/20 Vision For The New Decade!
2025 – 365 Day Journal
Document Your Journey!

Living Proverb #1835: "You're smart! In regard to doing something, don't be afraid to keep your own counsel, because nothing was ever the right way of doing something, until someone successfully did it, and then it became the right way. You're smart! Go right ahead!"

Gain 20/20 Vision For The New Decade!
2025 – 365 Day Journal
Document Your Journey!

Living Proverb #1836: "Don't be afraid to be uncommon, and to acknowledge the fact that you are uncommon, because only through your acknowledgement of the fact that you are uncommon, will you be able to offer and give properly your uncommon gift to the world."

Gain 20/20 Vision For The New Decade!
2025 – 365 Day Journal
Document Your Journey!

Living Proverb #1837: "When you submit your will to God's will, there's nothing in Earth, Heaven, or in Hell that can withstand the force of that *will*, because when you submit to God's will, it shall come to pass. You can do all things through Christ, which strengthens you."

Gain 20/20 Vision For The New Decade!
2025 – 365 Day Journal
Document Your Journey!

Living Proverb #1838: "Never replace the *brand* of God, for the brand of man. God brands your heart. Man attempts to brand your mind. Take time to renew your mind with the Word of God, and thereby, *brand* your life."

Gain 20/20 Vision For The New Decade!
2025 – 365 Day Journal
Document Your Journey!

Living Proverb #1846: "When you truly commit to accomplishing God's will for your life, and you're willing to fight for it, no matter what, God will stop the clock for you! In fact, He will *turn back time* in order to help you finish what He's already predetermined for you to finish."

Gain 20/20 Vision For The New Decade!
2025 – 365 Day Journal
Document Your Journey!

Living Proverb #1847: "Start the day with praise and worship, and you'll start the day as an unequivocal victor and success! There's nothing that can withstand the force of sincere praise and worship!"

Gain 20/20 Vision For The New Decade!
2025 – 365 Day Journal
Document Your Journey!

Living Proverb #1848: "Without action there's no satisfaction. Without action there are no results. Without action there's no fulfilment of the promise!"

Gain 20/20 Vision For The New Decade!
2025 – 365 Day Journal
Document Your Journey!

Living Proverb #1849: "If it seems like your blessing has been 'a-long-time-coming', then, what God is doing is allowing you to 'walk-it-out', so that when you finish obtaining that blessing, you will know what you're talking about, and no one, nowhere, at anytime will be able to take it."

Gain 20/20 Vision For The New Decade!
2025 – 365 Day Journal
Document Your Journey!

Living Proverb #1850: "Be your own cheerleader! Only you are responsible to know exactly what it takes to motivate you. Don't put that responsibility on anyone else. Be your own cheerleader. You will be more consistently motivated."

Gain 20/20 Vision For The New Decade!
2025 – 365 Day Journal
Document Your Journey!

Living Proverb #1851: "Success takes what it takes. Don't be afraid or discouraged by the time that it takes to succeed. You don't have anything else to do, but fail, if you don't go for it! So, *go for it*! Success will be 'right-on-time' if you simply go for it!"

Gain 20/20 Vision For The New Decade!
2025 – 365 Day Journal
Document Your Journey!

Living Proverb #1854: "Success is not overnight. However, success is every night. To achieve and maintain success takes every day and every night."

Gain 20/20 Vision For The New Decade!
2025 – 365 Day Journal
Document Your Journey!

Living Proverb #1855: "Pay off your small credit cards as soon as possible, because the 'small foxes' spoil the credit."

Gain 20/20 Vision For The New Decade!
2025 – 365 Day Journal
Document Your Journey!

Living Proverb #1857: "The only thing that determines whether something is one person's junk or another person's treasure is the degree of thankfulness or the lack thereof."

Gain 20/20 Vision For The New Decade!
2025 – 365 Day Journal
Document Your Journey!

Living Proverb #1863: "People who have extra *did extra*."

Gain 20/20 Vision For The New Decade!
2025 – 365 Day Journal
Document Your Journey!

Living Proverb #1864: "No one person or group of people has the monopoly on good ideas. The only person who has a monopoly on good ideas is the one who takes action on those ideas, because every time a new idea comes forth, it resets the standard of what is possible."

Gain 20/20 Vision For The New Decade!
2025 – 365 Day Journal
Document Your Journey!

Living Proverb #1869: "After you've had a long day, the habit of meditating the Word of God will reconstitute you into a full, whole, strong man or woman."

Gain 20/20 Vision For The New Decade!
2025 – 365 Day Journal
Document Your Journey!

Living Proverb #1871: "Do not be conformed to this world and its way of thinking. Rather, be a transformer! Transform your mind by the Word of God! Meditate God's Word daily. Read the Word! Speak the Word! Live out the Word! You will truly be a transformer!"

Gain 20/20 Vision For The New Decade!
2025 – 365 Day Journal
Document Your Journey!

Living Proverb #1873: "The reasons to praise the Lord just keep multiplying hour by hour; day by day; and year by year! Take time to count the many reasons to praise Him today! You will feel much better!"

Gain 20/20 Vision For The New Decade!
2025 – 365 Day Journal
Document Your Journey!

Living Proverb #1875: "As you feed upon God's Word, by actively, intentionally using it as a tool to advance in life, you will discover new levels of productivity."

Gain 20/20 Vision For The New Decade!
2025 – 365 Day Journal
Document Your Journey!

Living Proverb #1878: "Read the Bible everyday. Pray everyday. Sing songs of worship to God everyday. There will be days when you will not clearly see your answer. However, because you have a habit of continual fellowship with God, He can lead you anyway."

Gain 20/20 Vision For The New Decade!
2025 – 365 Day Journal
Document Your Journey!

Living Proverb #1879: "Unreleased potential fails to benefit you."

Gain 20/20 Vision For The New Decade!
2025 – 365 Day Journal
Document Your Journey!

Living Proverb #1881: "If you're patient enough, and you give yourself enough learning time, you can eliminate begging. Begging is a result of lack. It's a result of lack of knowledge, lack of resources, lack of 'know-how', and lack of ability. Gain knowledge to eliminate begging."

Gain 20/20 Vision For The New Decade!
2025 – 365 Day Journal
Document Your Journey!

Living Proverb #1886: "When God tells you to do something, just obey. It doesn't have to be pretty for it to be effective. If He tells you to do it, just quickly obey."

Gain 20/20 Vision For The New Decade!
2025 – 365 Day Journal
Document Your Journey!

Living Proverb #1888: "In regard to self-improvement, commit the cultivation of godly virtues of your heart to God through the Word, prayer, worship, and fasting. Cultivate your gifts, talents, and skills to your own personal discipline and hard work."

Gain 20/20 Vision For The New Decade!
2025 – 365 Day Journal
Document Your Journey!

Living Proverb #1891: "The key to maintaining joy is to focus on the good, and to be thankful."

Gain 20/20 Vision For The New Decade!
2025 – 365 Day Journal
Document Your Journey!

Living Proverb #1892: "There's safety in following in someone else's footsteps. However, it's better to have your own boots! Be wise enough to strike out on your own path! Make your own footsteps. Make your own path. Follow others footsteps, but wear your *own boots*!"

Gain 20/20 Vision For The New Decade!
2025 – 365 Day Journal
Document Your Journey!

Living Proverb #1893: "Be sober. Be vigilant. Don't let your emotions get the best of your head."

Gain 20/20 Vision For The New Decade!
2025 – 365 Day Journal
Document Your Journey!

Living Proverb #1894: "Without discipline, there is no release. Without the release of the anointing, there is no wealth!"

Gain 20/20 Vision For The New Decade!
2025 – 365 Day Journal
Document Your Journey!

Living Proverb #1895: "Vision provokes passion! Through passion purpose is obtained. Passion is the ignition for movement. Without movement nothing is accomplished."

Gain 20/20 Vision For The New Decade!
2025 – 365 Day Journal
Document Your Journey!

Living Proverb #1897: "Some of the greatest blessings come out of service."

Gain 20/20 Vision For The New Decade!
2025 – 365 Day Journal
Document Your Journey!

Living Proverb #1899: "The best way to mark your calendar is through achieved goals. Keep your calendar full by setting high, achievable goals, and keeping on achieving them!"

Gain 20/20 Vision For The New Decade!
2025 – 365 Day Journal
Document Your Journey!

Living Proverb #1901: "God wants to bless us, so that we'll help Him accomplish His purpose in the earth. We deprive Him of pleasure, and hinder His plan, when we fail to achieve."

Gain 20/20 Vision For The New Decade!
2025 – 365 Day Journal
Document Your Journey!

Living Proverb #1902: "The only thing that stands between you and your greatest dreams coming true is *work*. The only thing that stands between you doing the work to obtain your greatest dreams is your *willingness* to do the work."

Gain 20/20 Vision For The New Decade!
2025 – 365 Day Journal
Document Your Journey!

Living Proverb #1903: "Unbroken focus is the key to your ultimate financial success. Unending distractions are the keys to your eventual financial destruction."

Gain 20/20 Vision For The New Decade!
2025 – 365 Day Journal
Document Your Journey!

Living Proverb #1906: "In business and in life, you cannot lie back on the beach and expect someone to *feed you grapes*! No! You have to go into your promised land, and cut down the grapes! Even if you have to bring them out on a staff on your shoulder!"

Gain 20/20 Vision For The New Decade!
2025 – 365 Day Journal
Document Your Journey!

Living Proverb #1913: "Everyone is a 'star' in someone else's sky. So, shine while you can. Make the most of your days and nights. Shine as bright as the Sun in the day. Give direction and guidance as the North Star in someone's night. Let your light so very much shine!"

Gain 20/20 Vision For The New Decade!
2025 – 365 Day Journal
Document Your Journey!

Living Proverb #1914: "Have a 'spiritual sandwich' everyday. Have a time of morning devotion and evening devotion. Talk to the Lord and praise Him in the middle of the day. You will never go hungry. You will be filled with the Spirit daily."

Gain 20/20 Vision For The New Decade!
2025 – 365 Day Journal
Document Your Journey!

Living Proverb #1915: "God is pleased with you today! You are the highlight of Heaven. Every morning you wake up He delights in you. He takes pleasure in your progress, and He takes pleasure in prospering you. You are the highlight of Heaven today!"

Gain 20/20 Vision For The New Decade!
2025 – 365 Day Journal
Document Your Journey!

Living Proverb #1916: "Singing praise and worship to God clears out all of the *cobwebs* out of your mind and heart. Make room for the Holy Ghost. Sing praise and worship onto God."

Gain 20/20 Vision For The New Decade!
2025 – 365 Day Journal
Document Your Journey!

Living Proverb #1917: "Singing daily is an *attitude lifter*!"

Gain 20/20 Vision For The New Decade!
2025 – 365 Day Journal
Document Your Journey!

Living Proverb #1919: "If God is able to bring you up, He's able to keep you up. It was Him that brought you up. Don't be afraid of whether success can last. If God brings you up, then He can keep you up all the days of your life!"

Gain 20/20 Vision For The New Decade!
2025 – 365 Day Journal
Document Your Journey!

Living Proverb #1920: "Regarding your field of dreams, you can't guarantee that if you build it, they will come, but you can guarantee that if you don't build it they won't come. Pursue your dreams. Take the chance. You only have one life to live. Successful people pursue dreams."

Gain 20/20 Vision For The New Decade!
2025 – 365 Day Journal
Document Your Journey!

Living Proverb #1922: "Who has ears to hear? Let them hear: you were born on purpose. You were born with a purpose. You are a significant shift that has changed the direction of the future of history! Now, fulfill yourself!"

Gain 20/20 Vision For The New Decade!
2025 – 365 Day Journal
Document Your Journey!

Living Proverb #1923: "Some characteristics are a matter of personality. Some characteristics are a matter of refinement. Success requires refinement of our personalities."

Gain 20/20 Vision For The New Decade!
2025 – 365 Day Journal
Document Your Journey!

Living Proverb #1926: "Determination, patience, and persistence are the keys to success. Determine your desired destination. Be patient in the process. Persist to the end, and you will obtain success."

Gain 20/20 Vision For The New Decade!
2025 – 365 Day Journal
Document Your Journey!

Living Proverb #1927: "Workers get paid by the hour. Producers get paid by the product. Workers earn a wage. Producers earn wealth."

Gain 20/20 Vision For The New Decade!
2025 – 365 Day Journal
Document Your Journey!

Living Proverb #1928: "Happiness is a weapon."

Gain 20/20 Vision For The New Decade!
2025 – 365 Day Journal
Document Your Journey!

Living Proverb #1929: "No matter how your critics try to fight you, always know that no one can fight what God has ordained. If God said, 'Yes', who else matter?"

Gain 20/20 Vision For The New Decade!
2025 – 365 Day Journal
Document Your Journey!

Living Proverb #1930: "Take all opportunities that advance you in the right direction."

Gain 20/20 Vision For The New Decade!
2025 – 365 Day Journal
Document Your Journey!

Living Proverb #1933: "Life takes courage."

Gain 20/20 Vision For The New Decade!
2025 – 365 Day Journal
Document Your Journey!

Living Proverb #1934: "Regarding money, excitement leads to spending. Patience leads to planning. Be strategic in your use of money. It will lead to an exciting result."

Gain 20/20 Vision For The New Decade!
2025 – 365 Day Journal
Document Your Journey!

Living Proverb #1935: "Pay for advisement, but keep your own counsel."

Gain 20/20 Vision For The New Decade!
2025 – 365 Day Journal
Document Your Journey!

Living Proverb #1936: "Always remember, you are the CEO of your own life. Pay for advice, but don't lose your status."

Gain 20/20 Vision For The New Decade!
2025 – 365 Day Journal
Document Your Journey!

Living Proverb #1938: "Ideas and concepts are how the 'West was won', and how business is run. Take time to appraise the tremendous creative and monetary value of your own ideas and concepts, and don't allow yourself to be swindled, hornswoggled, or bamboozled by others."

Gain 20/20 Vision For The New Decade!
2025 – 365 Day Journal
Document Your Journey!

Living Proverb #1939: "Excitement begets spending. Patience begets planning."

Gain 20/20 Vision For The New Decade!
2025 – 365 Day Journal
Document Your Journey!

Living Proverb #1940: "The way to succeed is to start with a burning, grand vision. Then, keep taking the necessary steps towards its fulfillment. It becomes clearer and clearer, as you take actions towards it. Then, seemingly, suddenly it will appear into full view."

Gain 20/20 Vision For The New Decade!
2025 – 365 Day Journal
Document Your Journey!

Living Proverb #1941: "When the saints prevail in prayer, the saints will prevail."

Gain 20/20 Vision For The New Decade!
2025 – 365 Day Journal
Document Your Journey!

Living Proverb #1942: "The best way to make money is to not spend money. There's a difference between an expense and an investment. Expenses are spent. Investments are a vested interest into your future. Invest money and reduce the instances of spending money."

Gain 20/20 Vision For The New Decade!
2025 – 365 Day Journal
Document Your Journey!

Living Proverb #1943: "Invest your money to make more money. Don't just spend money randomly."

Gain 20/20 Vision For The New Decade!
2025 – 365 Day Journal
Document Your Journey!

Living Proverb #1944: "Don't start spending before you start counting!"

Gain 20/20 Vision For The New Decade!
2025 – 365 Day Journal
Document Your Journey!

Living Proverb #1945: "Don't worry about the time that it takes to do what's required to obtain what's desired. Progress is progressive."

Gain 20/20 Vision For The New Decade!
2025 – 365 Day Journal
Document Your Journey!

Living Proverb #1946: "Life is full of reality. It's good to have a dream. The just shall live by his or her faith!"

Gain 20/20 Vision For The New Decade!
2025 – 365 Day Journal
Document Your Journey!

Living Proverb #1949: "Life is a trip! Your attitude will determine how you take it!"

Gain 20/20 Vision For The New Decade!
2025 – 365 Day Journal
Document Your Journey!

Living Proverb #1950: "Happiness and joy are a matter of choice. It's a matter of attitude. It's a matter of the heart. It's not a matter of the circumstances. Don't let anything or anyone take your joy. Happiness is a matter of the heart. It's not a matter of the circumstances."

Gain 20/20 Vision For The New Decade!
2025 – 365 Day Journal
Document Your Journey!

Living Proverb #1952: "You're paid to solve problems. So, if you run away from problems, you run away from your *paycheck*."

Gain 20/20 Vision For The New Decade!
2025 – 365 Day Journal
Document Your Journey!

Living Proverb #1953: "The willingness to go to any lawful extreme is the price of extreme success."

Gain 20/20 Vision For The New Decade!
2025 – 365 Day Journal
Document Your Journey!

Living Proverb #1954: "Drown out the voices of adversaries, opposition, and criticism by the force of your productivity. They may continue to talk, but you will no longer be distracted by their influence, because you will be too absorbed in succeeding. Just keep producing!"

Gain 20/20 Vision For The New Decade!
2025 – 365 Day Journal
Document Your Journey!

Living Proverb #1955: "Keep sowing seed toward the future, and you will have both a future and a harvest."

Gain 20/20 Vision For The New Decade!
2025 – 365 Day Journal
Document Your Journey!

Living Proverb #1956: "Regarding business, no single company or organization fully owns the entire market. Otherwise, they wouldn't continue marketing."

Gain 20/20 Vision For The New Decade!
2025 – 365 Day Journal
Document Your Journey!

Living Proverb #1957: "Don't fight getting older. Rather, focus on getting better every day of every year. Live everyday with intentionality, so that you are daily fulfilling your God-given purpose. You will then have a greater sense of satisfaction as the years go by."

Gain 20/20 Vision For The New Decade!
2025 – 365 Day Journal
Document Your Journey!

Living Proverb #1958: "Insist on being the best, and make no allowances for the lower part of your nature."

Gain 20/20 Vision For The New Decade!
2025 – 365 Day Journal
Document Your Journey!

Living Proverb #1960: "Regarding business, business is not black-and-white. Business is green."

Gain 20/20 Vision For The New Decade!
2025 – 365 Day Journal
Document Your Journey!

Living Proverb #1961: "It pays to live right. It pays to live holy. It pays to live for Jesus Christ as Lord and Savior, because when it gets all the way down to the 'nitty-gritty', I just want to see that *Golden city*!"

Gain 20/20 Vision For The New Decade!
2025 – 365 Day Journal
Document Your Journey!

Living Proverb #1962: "The Lord is working on your behalf. The future is brighter than you may now perceive. Keep looking up. The Sun is shining in your direction!"

Gain 20/20 Vision For The New Decade!
2025 – 365 Day Journal
Document Your Journey!

Living Proverb #1964: "Don't stress-out. Rather, press into prayer."

Gain 20/20 Vision For The New Decade!
2025 – 365 Day Journal
Document Your Journey!

Living Proverb #1965: "Sincere appreciation is always appreciated."

Gain 20/20 Vision For The New Decade!
2025 – 365 Day Journal
Document Your Journey!

Living Proverb #1966: "If it can be done, it should be done. You don't know what can be done, until you try. Don't say what can't be done, until you try. If it can be done, it should be done. You can do it!"

Gain 20/20 Vision For The New Decade!
2025 – 365 Day Journal
Document Your Journey!

Living Proverb #1967: "Wherever you are, you should learn something."

Gain 20/20 Vision For The New Decade!
2025 – 365 Day Journal
Document Your Journey!

Living Proverb #1968: "It pays to be prepared and prompt. It costs to be lax and late."

Gain 20/20 Vision For The New Decade!
2025 – 365 Day Journal
Document Your Journey!

Living Proverb #1969: "Regarding rest, even the Sun goes down at the end of the day. Take time to get your rest."

Gain 20/20 Vision For The New Decade!
2025 – 365 Day Journal
Document Your Journey!

Living Proverb #1970: "Once you make the decision to solve a problem, it's no longer a problem. It becomes a challenge. Go forward courageously with the commitment to address the challenge. You will win as the champion!"

Gain 20/20 Vision For The New Decade!
2025 – 365 Day Journal
Document Your Journey!

Living Proverb #1971: "Good things come to those who *stay awake!*"

Gain 20/20 Vision For The New Decade!
2025 – 365 Day Journal
Document Your Journey!

Living Proverb #1972: "Anytime a person is doing too much talking, pay close attention not to pay too much attention."

Gain 20/20 Vision For The New Decade!
2025 – 365 Day Journal
Document Your Journey!

Living Proverb #1974: "No complaints. Just action!"

Gain 20/20 Vision For The New Decade!
2025 – 365 Day Journal
Document Your Journey!

Living Proverb #1975: "The childish complain and remain. The mature respond and go beyond."

Gain 20/20 Vision For The New Decade!
2025 – 365 Day Journal
Document Your Journey!

Living Proverb #1976: "After some time, you mature enough to realize that you are not perfect. The other person is not perfect either. Yet, we each are perfectly ourselves. Neither person is weird. We're just all *fascinatingly different!*"

Gain 20/20 Vision For The New Decade!
2025 – 365 Day Journal
Document Your Journey!

Living Proverb #1977: "Regarding timing, it's always good to know when to say *when*."

Gain 20/20 Vision For The New Decade!
2025 – 365 Day Journal
Document Your Journey!

Living Proverb #1978: "People's behavior in your past informs you of their merits to be a part of your *future*."

Gain 20/20 Vision For The New Decade!
2025 – 365 Day Journal
Document Your Journey!

Living Proverb #1979: "Regarding destiny, when God gives you an opportunity to escape the land of mediocrity, never look back, because looking back could be deadly to your dreams. Remember *Lot's wife!*"

Gain 20/20 Vision For The New Decade!
2025 – 365 Day Journal
Document Your Journey!

Living Proverb #1982: "We're the *'manifestation generation.'* We're not prevented by previous limitations. We have been empowered to change our situations. We are the head and not the tail. We are blessed above all nations. You are a part of the *manifestation generation!*"

Gain 20/20 Vision For The New Decade!
2025 – 365 Day Journal
Document Your Journey!

Living Proverb #1983: "I declare God's richest and best blessings upon you now! In Jesus name, amen."

Gain 20/20 Vision For The New Decade!
2025 – 365 Day Journal
Document Your Journey!

Living Proverb #1984: "No one can stop anyone who takes the time to transform his or her mind. You can't stop an acorn from becoming an oak tree if it's transformed. You can't keep it in the ground. No one can stop anyone who takes time to transform his or her mind."

Gain 20/20 Vision For The New Decade!
2025 – 365 Day Journal
Document Your Journey!

Living Proverb #1985: "God's eyes are '*running to and fro*' throughout the earth, looking for someone to bless. Give Him something to bless by obeying His commandment to be fruitful, creative, and productive. His angels are informing Him of those who are at the *peak of ripeness*!"

Gain 20/20 Vision For The New Decade!
2025 – 365 Day Journal
Document Your Journey!

Living Proverb #1986: "Let excellence be the signature of your work today. Show people who you are by what you do and the attitude you do it in. Represent the high standards of God in all that you do. You are a child of The Most High God."

Gain 20/20 Vision For The New Decade!
2025 – 365 Day Journal
Document Your Journey!

Living Proverb #1987: "Our differences in tastes, inclinations, and passions regarding life and career choice are a testament of the Creator's creativity and His special consideration of us."

Gain 20/20 Vision For The New Decade!
2025 – 365 Day Journal
Document Your Journey!

Living Proverb #1992: "Regarding opposition, does the elephant feel the kicking of the ant? Do not be moved by your adversaries. Just keep on marching forward!"

Gain 20/20 Vision For The New Decade!
2025 – 365 Day Journal
Document Your Journey!

Living Proverb #1994: "No matter what life tries to put on you, don't let it take what God gave you!"

Gain 20/20 Vision For The New Decade!
2025 – 365 Day Journal
Document Your Journey!

Living Proverb #1996: "Even those who demand perfection are not perfect."

Gain 20/20 Vision For The New Decade!
2025 – 365 Day Journal
Document Your Journey!

Living Proverb #1997: "Regarding giving and receiving, the carnal, fleshly nature seeks to bind you with cords of indebtedness. True love gives wings, not strings. True love is a free gift."

Gain 20/20 Vision For The New Decade!
2025 – 365 Day Journal
Document Your Journey!

Living Proverb #2002: "You have to keep doing what you *need* to do, so you can keep doing what you *want* to do."

Gain 20/20 Vision For The New Decade!
2025 – 365 Day Journal
Document Your Journey!

Living Proverb #2021: "Being able to see beyond where you are, empowers you to go to where you want to be."

Gain 20/20 Vision For The New Decade!
2025 – 365 Day Journal
Document Your Journey!

www.ingramcontent.com/pod-product-compliance
Lightning Source LLC
Chambersburg PA
CBHW072146070526
44585CB00015B/1019